THE CHIMAERA

MONSTERS OF MYTHOLOGY

25 VOLUMES

Hellenic

Amycus
Anteus
The Calydonian Boar
Cerberus
Chimaera
The Cyclopes
The Dragon of Boeotia
The Furies
Geryon
Harpalyce
Hecate
The Hydra
Ladon
Medusa
The Minotaur
The Nemean Lion
Procrustes
Scylla and Charybdis
The Sirens
The Spear-birds
The Sphinx

Norse

Fafnir
Fenris

Celtic

Drabne of Dole
Pig's Ploughman

MONSTERS OF MYTHOLOGY

THE CHIMAERA

Bernard Evslin

CHELSEA HOUSE PUBLISHERS

New York New Haven Philadelphia

— 1988 —

EDITOR
Jennifer Caldwell

ART DIRECTOR
Giannella Garrett

PICTURE RESEARCHER
Ann Levy

DESIGNER
Victoria Tomaselli

CREATIVE DIRECTOR
Harold Steinberg

First Printing

Library of Congress Cataloging-in-Publication Data

Evslin, Bernard.
The Chimaera.

(Monsters of mythology)
Summary: Young hero Bellerophon sets out to
conquer the fire-breathing chimera and win
the hand of Queen Anteia.
1. Chimera (Greek mythology)—Juvenile literature.
2. Bellerophon (Greek mythology)—Juvenile literature.
[1. Chimera (Greek mythology) 2. Bellerophon (Greek
mythology) 3. Mythology, Greek] I. Title.
II. Series: Evslin, Bernard. Monsters of mythology.
BL820.C57E95   1988   398.2'1'0938   87-14597

ISBN 1-55546-244-8

Printed in Singapore

For our bonus grandson
JESSE CLINTON
and a handsome bonus he is.

Characters

Monster

The Chimaera
(ky MEE ruh)
    A dreadful creature composed of lion, goat, and serpent, in the worst possible combination

Gods

Zeus
(ZOOS)
    King of the Gods

Poseidon
(poh SY duhn)
    Zeus's brother, God of the Sea

Demeter
(duh MEE tuhr)
    Goddess of the Harvest

Mortals

Bellerophon
(buh LAIR uh fuhn)
A young hero; son of Poseidon

Eurymede
(yoo RIM uh dee)
Bellerophon's mother; dead, but still active

Melicertes
(mehl uh SUR teez)
King of Corinth

Anteia
(an TY yuh)
Queen of Tiryns; Bellerophon's cousin

Iobates
(eye OB a teez)
Anteia's father; king of Lycia

Proetus
(proh EE tuhs)
Anteia's husband; king of Tiryns

Thallo
(THUH loh)
A poet

Pirate Captain
A sea-bandit of Lycia

The Oracle
A blind seer

Animals

Sea Mist
A great gray stallion

Pegasus
(PEG uh suhs)
A winged white horse

Other horses of Corinth
Owned by Melicertes and trained to be lethal

Contents

CHAPTER I

Monster and Monarch   1

CHAPTER II

The Smallest Archer   5

CHAPTER III

The Horse-Breaker   11

CHAPTER IV

The Warning   17

CHAPTER V

The Tormented Land   21

CHAPTER VI

The Blind Seer   25

CHAPTER VII

The Mad King   31

CHAPTER VIII

A Gathering Doom   35

CHAPTER IX

Hooves of Death   39

CHAPTER X

Anteia   47

CHAPTER XI

The Hunt Begins   55

CHAPTER XII

Dangerous Passage   59

CHAPTER XIII

The Ghost Returns   67

CHAPTER XIV

The Winged Horse   71

CHAPTER XV

The Chimaera   81

1

Monster and Monarch

t was a clear, hot morning, but the Lycians were frozen with horror. The Chimaera had appeared in their skies and was hovering overhead. One chieftain tried to hearten his people.

"It won't land here," he said. "It's on its way to Corinth. For monsters are sent to punish wicked kings. And who is more wicked than Melicertes?"

While he was still insisting that the monster was going elsewhere, it swooped down on the village and devoured the entire population—men, women, and children; then it proceeded to the next village and ate everyone there, but more slowly. Whereupon, it flew heavily toward the mountains, and didn't go to Corinth at all.

As for the hopeful chieftain, he had attacked the Chimaera as soon as it touched ground, struck one blow with his sword and disappeared down the smoky gullet before he had time to realize how little he knew about monsters.

Now, as the Chimaera flies eastward, we go west—to that bridge of land known as Corinth that connects the land masses of Arcadia and Boeotia. This rich kingdom was ruled by Melicertes the Malevolent, whose reputation for evil had spread to all the lands of the Middle Sea basin.

Melicertes bred horses.

Melicertes bred horses; he fattened his coffers by betting vast sums on himself in chariot races. This kind of sport was the favorite pastime of ancient royalty, and Melicertes never lost a race. Nor did he depend on the speed of his horses; he had trained them to be killers.

Whenever a rival chariot threatened to pass his, Melicertes would whistle in a certain way; his steeds would swerve in their traces and attack the other team like a pack of wolves, throwing them into a panic, causing them to bolt frantically in the wrong direction. Then, bugling and snorting and tossing their manes, the Corinthian team would gallop off again, pulling the royal chariot across the finish line.

Early in the history of these races, one defeated driver claimed a foul. But protests were cut short by the sudden death of the complainant. An arrow sticking out of his throat aroused certain suspicions, but no one was prepared to accuse the king of foul play, nor did anyone ever again protest a Melicertes victory.

The king had brought his horses to this pitch of viciousness by raising them on a diet of raw meat. As soon as the foals stopped drinking mare's milk, they were fed bloody hunks of beef and pork. When they became yearlings, they were introduced to forbidden food. Into the stalls of the gigantic colts were thrown those unfortunate enough to have offended the king, who was easily offended. This diet also saved the cost of jailers and hangmen. Every crime was punishable by death; a crime was whatever the king said it was; and there was a steady supply of human flesh for the royal stables.

So the king prospered as a charioteer; his only problem was keeping help. But he solved this in his own way. Since his particular administration of justice left many orphans, he formed them into a labor pool to be tapped whenever he needed a new groom or stable boy.

2

The Smallest Archer

elicertes was about forty-five, and had already run through nine wives. No one knew what he did with them; they simply vanished. As soon as he discarded one, he would choose another—no older than eighteen and always the most beautiful maiden in the land. No girl dared refuse him, and if she were so inclined her parents would overrule her. For anyone who crossed the king became horse fodder.

Naturally, people wondered what happened to the ex-wives, but didn't dare discuss it. In fact, they hardly dared *think* about it. For they feared the king so much that they believed he could read minds at a distance—that anyone who entertained any critical opinion of royal behavior would soon find himself being fed to the horses.

For all the secrecy and terror that surrounded Melicertes, however, there was one rumor that stubbornly refused to fade away. It was said that some years before, after only five wives, the king had been refused by a girl whom he wished to make his sixth. She couldn't marry him, she had said, because she was already the bride of the sea. A year before, Poseidon had ridden in on a tidal wave, swept her up, and carried her away, then returned her to her village the next day. When the king refused to believe her, she produced an infant, who, she said, was Poseidon's son. Melicertes still refused to accept her story, and insisted that she be his. She fled. He pursued. She raced to the edge of a cliff and flung herself into the sea. The king, enraged, was about to throw the baby in after her, but something stopped him.

"I'm not quite sure there are such things as gods," he said to himself. "I've never seen any, and I dislike the idea that anything can be more powerful than I am. Nevertheless, I'm not certain that they don't exist, and there's no use taking unnecessary chances. If there should be a sea god named Poseidon, he might be annoyed with me. And if this child is really his, as she said, I'll only make things worse by drowning it. My kingdom is an isthmus, after all, and a sea god, no doubt, can whistle up a storm whenever he pleases and bury this strip of land under fathoms of water. So I think I'll assume that Poseidon exists and try to appease him by raising his brat as my own."

So the king had the gray-eyed babe taken to the palace and dropped among a horde of other motherless princes and princesses who romped through the royal park, wild as bear cubs. The little boy was nameless at first. Then the other children began to call him Bellerophon.

He was as friendly and affectionate as a puppy. His one ambition was to grow big enough to join the violent play of the older children. They played outdoors from morning till night, and their favorite game was "War."

Each morning, the biggest and strongest appointed themselves chiefs and chose up sides. Armed with wooden swords and blunted javelins, the little warriors would then rage over the fields and into the woods in whatever form of the game they had picked that day—"Ambush," "Pitched Battle," or "Siege." They played rough. Any bruise or cut was a badge of honor, and no child ever complained. The king approved of these games. They were

The children played outdoors
from morning till night, and
their favorite game was "War."

good training for the real thing. He chose his young officers from among his sons. He also watched for symptoms of dangerous ambition. A prince who showed signs of aspiring to kingship simply vanished, and no one asked why. The Corinthians had learned not to.

Now, little Bellerophon couldn't wait to be chosen in a game of "War." He hung about the outskirts of the battles, watching everything, picking favorites among the players, and studying their weapon play. Finally, one day, a boy slightly older than he sprained his ankle, leaving the sides uneven. Bellerophon's heart began to gallop as the chiefs counted their troops. He almost burst with joy when one of them beckoned to him and ordered: "You! Get out here!"

Bellerophon was prepared. Ever since he could toddle he had been getting himself ready for this glorious day. He had made

himself a little bow and a quiver of arrows. The chief guffawed when he saw the tiny bow and the arrows no bigger than darts.

"What are you going to do with that?" he cried. "Shoot grasshoppers?"

Bellerophon grinned at him, and darted off, so swiftly that it seemed he had been swallowed by the meadow. He lay in the tall grass amid the buzz and click of insects. Notching his arrow to his bow, he pointed it straight up, and waited.

It was a drowsy place, full of sleepy sounds. Bellerophon was lying on his back, but he had never felt more awake. For the enemy's natural line of advance was across this meadow, and he knew that he was invisible. He waited. Then he heard someone yelling. He raised himself enough to take a quick peek, then sank back into the grass.

They were coming—in a long skirmish line. The grass trembled; insects departed. He drew back his arrow until the bow was bent double. And when the charging boy stumbled over him, stared down in astonishment, and then raised his wooden sword, Bellerophon released the bowstring. His arrow hit the attacker under the chin. Had it worn a sharp head it would have pierced the boy's throat. As it was, it knocked him to the ground, making him gasp for breath.

"You're dead!" cried Bellerophon. "Take yourself out."

The fallen boy picked himself up and staggered away, dazed. Bellerophon snatched up his arrow and notched it again—just in time. Someone else was coming. He shot him too. Then another. And another. Nestling like an adder in the meadow grass, he stung fifteen of the enemy with his little arrows, knocking them out of the game, and sealing victory for his side.

It was upon this day that he earned his name, Bellerophon, which meant "archer."

3

The Horse-Breaker

Poseidon, it is said, created the first horse as a gift for Demeter, and had always loved the animal. For himself he kept a string of white-maned stallions, which he rode at full gallop when the sea was rough. So it was that all his sons were ardent horsemen, could gentle the most vicious steed, and ride anything that moved. And now his smallest son was growing up among the mob of children sired by Melicertes.

Bellerophon was the youngest of this child swarm and different in other ways. They were not especially unkind to him, his adopted brothers and sisters, but they didn't completely accept him either. Bellerophon didn't let this bother him, though. While delighted when they played with him, he was nevertheless quite satisfied with his own company when left alone. In fact, he welcomed these hours of solitude, for he was making certain plans, which he preferred to keep to himself.

These schemes became the pivot of his lonely hours, and, finally, the theme of his young life. What happened was that he had become fascinated by the king's horses and had determined to ride them.

One big meadow held a stand of apple trees . . .
and Bellerophon had chosen this place for his own.

Paddock and stables had never been declared off limits to the royal children. No one ever dreamed of going anywhere near the man-eating horses if he could help it. This paddock was no small fenced area. It was an open range, acres of grassland girded by the great circular track where the chariot races were run. The stallions roamed as freely as a wild herd; actually, they were almost wild, broken only to chariot work and obeying only the king.

One big meadow held a stand of apple trees, however, and Bellerophon had chosen this place for his own. He could climb

12

like a squirrel. In a flash, he was off the ground, up a trunk and balancing on a huge limb. Here he would perch for hours, watching the horses—gazing rapturously as they ran free, studying them intently when the king came out to work them.

The boy was a natural mimic. He amused himself by imitating the call of lark and thrush and the hectoring crow. He also taught himself to whistle exactly as the king did when summoning the horses or ordering them to attack.

All this time, an intention was ripening within him—crowding his heart, following him into the night, and painting pictures on the walls of sleep. Finally, one day, the idea hatched.

He waited in his tree, trying to stifle his impatience until the king had finished his morning's work with the horses and departed. The boy filled his pouch with apples, waiting until he was sure the king was out of earshot. Then he whistled the piercing whistle that meant "Come!"

The nearest horse, a huge reddish brown colt, swiveled the keg of its head and rolled its eyes. The boy whistled again. The horse arched its neck, whisked its tail, and pranced sideways, then turned and trotted toward the sound.

The horse came under the apple tree. Lightly as a leaf, the boy dropped down onto its back. But the colt had never been ridden. It bolted through the orchard, brushing against tree trunks, trying to knock the boy off. But Bellerophon drew one leg up, then the other, and finally sat cross-legged, riding this awful power as comfortably as a petrel bobbing on a stormy sea.

The colt burst through the orchard and entered the open meadow—bucking, sunfishing, landing jarringly on stiff legs, trying to get rid of its weird little burden. The boy felt no fear. This was where he belonged. Not for a moment did he consider that he might be thrown, smashing his head against a rock; or that the great jaws might catch his leg and tear it off; or that the furious horse might roll over on him, crushing him beneath its enormous weight.

No, nothing bad would happen. They were bound in a dance. The boy's small body was adjusting itself to the huge one.

They were connected by a secret bond, throbbing with life. The colt didn't know it yet. It was slower to know things. But it would learn. It had to. He loved the animal too much for it not to become aware.

The colt landed jarringly on stiff legs, trying to get rid of its weird little burden.

He perched on the raging animal and laughed with joy. The colt bugled suddenly, as if answering his laughter, then reared on its hind legs, pawing the air with its forehooves. Bellerophon clung to its mane. The horse came down with a jolt, stood on braced forelegs, and kicked out its back hooves in a terrific whiplash movement. But the boy was part of the horse now; he could not be thrown.

The colt's neck was satiny with sweat, wrapping the boy in its fragrance. The animal's strength was entering him, nourishing his courage, tuning his reflexes. He pulled an apple from his pouch, clasped the horse's neck with his legs, and slid around, hanging upside down with his face under the horse's mouth. He thrust the apple between its huge teeth, and twisted away, perching again on its wide back.

The beast ate the sweet fruit. It stood stock still, crunching. Bellerophon leaped off, stood before the animal and thrust another apple into its jaws, then another. The great, glossy wild eyes looked into his. The big head sank. The velvet lips began to nuzzle at him, searching for apples.

The boy turned his back and began to walk away. The colt reached again, seized the belt of his tunic between its teeth, swung the boy off the ground, and flipped him into the air. Bellerophon turned a backward somersault and landed on the horse's back. He stood there for a moment, laughing. When he slid to riding position, the colt trotted off.

The sun was sinking behind them now and cast a great humped shadow that swung before them as they moved toward the rest of the herd.

4

The Warning

For the next year, Bellerophon visited the horses every day, and, one by one, mastered them all. He was able to do all this without being observed, for everyone shunned the royal paddock except the king and whatever stable help had survived the month.

Finally, however, another craving began to gnaw at the boy. He found himself wanting everyone to know that he alone could manage these terrifying animals. He pictured himself riding toward the other children just as they were choosing up sides for the war game—riding in on one of the great stallions, vaulting on and off its back at a full gallop, doing handstands on its back, sliding around its neck and feeding it apples, performing all these marvelous tricks as the other children gaped in wonder.

How they would admire him! How they would fight among themselves for the privilege of being on his team. Why, he would be named a squadron of cavalry all by himself. His heart swelled with these visions of glory; it got so that he couldn't sleep.

One night he grew so excited that he sat bolt upright in bed, preparing to dash out into the moonlight, race to the stables, and ride one of the horses right up the palace steps and among the sleeping children.

"How wonderful," he whispered to himself. "They'll think they're dreaming, but then realize they're awake. I'll laugh and ride away, and in the morning they won't know whether I'm a dream or not."

Moonlight shifted through the arrow-slit that served as a window for his little chamber. The light curdled, thickened, lengthened itself—became a tall milky form. It lifted its arms and threw back its cowl. He saw a fall of dark hair and a pale sliver of face.

"Who are you?" he whispered.

"I am your mother."

"She's dead."

"I am her ghost."

"Why do you come?" he asked.

"I love you."

"But you're dead."

"Love outlasts death. It is what troubles our repose and makes us walk the earth again."

"Why haven't you come before?" asked Bellerophon.

"I am permitted to appear to you only when you are to be warned," said the ghost. "Hush now, and listen. I can stay only a brief time and must speak my message only once."

> I am your mother,
> a bride of the sea.
> You have no other,
> only me.

"Who is my father, then?" asked the boy. "Is it Melicertes?"

> Not Melicertes,
> of a certainty.
> Your father,
> rather,
> is Lord of the Sea.

"Poseidon?" cried the boy. "Master of Tides? Who created the horse?"

>Indeed, 'twas he
>who made the horse,
>and gave you mastery.
>But that skill you must hide
>oh Son of the Tide.
>Let no one know
>how well you ride.

"But why, mother? I'm proud of it."
"That pride can be fatal, my boy," said the ghost.

>Hide, hide,
>hide your pride;
>let no one know
>how well you ride.
>Or the killer king
>will do again
>what he loves to do,
>And the royal ax will fall on you.

The boy sat silently.
"Do you understand?"
"Yes."
"Will you heed my words?"
"Yes . . . yes. Why are you fading?"
"I am leaving," said the ghost.
"No! Please! Stay!"
"Will you come again?"
"Perhaps. Farewell, my lovely boy. Farewell!"

She faded, vanished. The boy's tear-stained face caught the last ghostly light. He had never cried before. He wiped his eyes angrily, and sat staring into the shadows.

5

The Tormented Land

f those unfortunate enough to encounter the Chimaera, few lived to tell about it. And those who did manage to escape while it was devouring their neighbors were so stupefied by terror that they were unable to describe the monster.

Some said it was half dragon, half ram. Others said it was a flying lion, but with an eagle's head. Still others spoke of a winged serpent. All agreed, however, that it was a combination of at least two huge beasts, that it flew, that it spat flame, and that it was capable of devouring an entire village at a single meal.

Sifting through all these tales after some four thousand years, it is now thought that the monster which plagued Lycia had a lion's head and chest, a lion's teeth and claws, and the torso of a giant goat, with a tail that became a serpent, giving the beast jaws at both ends. It had leathery wings like a dragon, and a dragon's ability to spit fire. Of all the monsters spawned since the beginning of time, the Chimaera had perhaps the biggest appetite and the smallest intelligence.

No one knew why the Chimaera had chosen Lycia as its hunting ground. But during the years when Bellerophon was growing up in Corinth, the monster nested in the Lycian mountains and devastated the hillside villages. Then, when the hills were eaten bare, it flew out to ravage the coastal towns.

The king, Iobates, a kindly man, was so bewildered and grief-stricken by what was happening to his once happy people that he thought of offering his own life to appease whatever god was punishing his land. His wife and daughters pleaded with him

not to sacrifice himself, but his decision grew stronger with each new report of a village destroyed. He was hesitating only because he couldn't decide which god would be the most likely to accept the sacrifice. Iobates consulted seven priests. Each of them named a different god or goddess, which left him more confused than ever.

"Since it's impossible to learn who's punishing us," he thought, "I'll go right to the top, and put myself to the sword at the altar of the Almighty Zeus, who rules all the gods."

He returned to the palace to bid farewell to his family, but his youngest daughter, Anteia, clutched him, crying, "No, father, you must not!"

"Indeed, I must," he said.

"No, no, please listen. A dream visited me last night. No ordinary one but a vision from on high. I saw a monster in the sky breathing fire. The thatched roofs were burning. People ran, screaming. The beast came lower. Then the clouds broke,

The king, Iobates, a kindly man, was bewildered and grief-stricken by what was happening.

and light poured down. It turned to a spear of light and pierced the body of the monster like a fisherman gaffing a fish. The monster turned into black smoke and vanished, leaving the sky clear. A voice spoke, saying, 'Tell your father not to despair. A hero is being prepared to slay the foul beast.' Then I woke. But father, father, I believe that vision, I believe that voice. You must have faith, for help is on its way.''

"A hero is being prepared to save us, is that what your voice said?'' asked the king.

"Yes.''

"Well,'' said Iobates. "Whoever's preparing him better do so quickly or there won't be anything for him to save.''

"Please, father, please. Have faith.''

Now, the king had six daughters, some of them quite silly, and he was not prone to put much stock in anything they said. But this youngest daughter, Anteia, was far brighter than her sisters, as well as more beautiful, and the king loved her very much. While not quite believing in her dream, he was moved by her tears, and promised her he would not sacrifice himself, at least not immediately.

"I'm grateful for one thing,'' he said to himself. "She is betrothed to the king of Tiryns, and while she's much too good for him, will at least be safe at his court. I'll hasten the marriage.''

6

The Blind Seer

uring the years that the boy Bellerophon was ripening into manhood, King Melicertes was ripening into madness. He had always been cruel, had always been ruthless to his ene-mies, but such traits were not unusual among the rulers of that time, when the words *king* and *tyrant* were virtually synonymous. Melicertes, perhaps, was more cruel than other kings—more ruthless, certainly more dramatic; his man-eating horses were notorious throughout the Middle Sea basin. But, of late, his sus-picions had grown into a frenzy.

He saw enemies everywhere and ordered so many execu-tions that he couldn't use his horses on his prisoners; they would have grown too fat to race. So he kept his ax-men busy, cutting off heads. Nevertheless, this wholesale butchery did not ease his fears. He couldn't shake off the feeling that he was threatened— by what or whom he did not know, but he knew the threat was growing.

Finally, Melicertes consulted an oracle, although he had never believed in them. Word had come to him of a man who had gained a reputation for holiness by plucking out his own eyes, so that, as he said, he might listen without distraction to what the gods were trying to say. People flocked to this man, and were amazed at the accuracy of his predictions.

Melicertes did not send for this oracle; he wanted to test him. He doffed his crown, cast off his rich garments, ordered his royal guard to stay behind, and, in the guise of an ordinary horse breeder, visited the blind seer.

The old man turned the empty sockets of his eyes upon him, and said, "You are welcome, king. What do you want to know?"

It was not the king's nature to allow himself to be impressed; he tried hard now not to be. "Ah, bah," he thought to himself, "so he knows I'm a king, is that remarkable? I can change my clothes, but I cannot cast off my royal bearing or muffle the impact of my regal personality. It is so powerful that even a blind man recognizes me."

Aloud, he said, "I've heard great things about you. You read the future, I understand, as clearly as though it has already happened."

"True," said the blind man. "In fact, our future is embedded in our past. How could it not be? Time is circular. Or, more accurately, our lives spiral around the fixed point of what we are. We are our own fate. We lift ourselves out of the darkness of pre-birth into a brief light, making and unmaking ourselves as we travel toward the final darkness."

"Very fine," said the king. "Actually, I don't have much of a head for philosophy. I prefer facts. Can you tell me who threatens me, and why?"

"There are so many 'whys,'" said the seer. "You have created a multitude of corpses, O king. If you were to multiply each corpse by the number of those who had loved that person, alive, you might calculate the number of potential assassins you have made for yourself. But numbers don't matter. Like all of us, you are allowed only one death, and should concern yourself only with the assassin who will succeed."

"Then there is one!" roared the king. "Who is he? Tell me quickly, on pain of death."

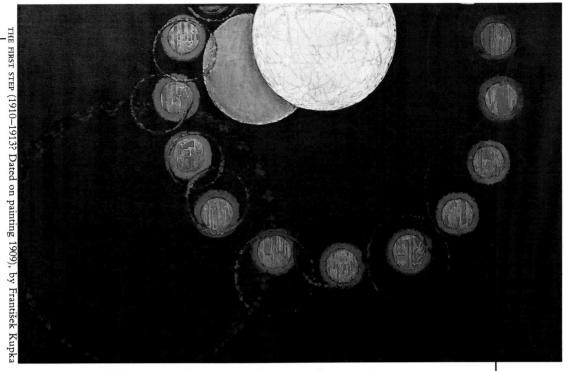

THE FIRST STEP (1910–1913? Dated on painting 1909), by František Kupka

*"Time is circular. . . . our lives spiral
around the fixed point of what we are."*

The blind man sighed and pointed to his empty sockets. "Do you really think I fear pain, O king? When I tore out my own eyes I freed myself from the fear of physical pain as I freed myself from the distractions of the visible world. You cannot threaten me."

"Please," whispered the king, "I implore you. I, who have never begged for anything in my life, am begging now. Tell me the name of my assassin."

"I can tell you this," said the oracle. "You have fashioned your own death. It waits for you. And will be presented to you by one who comes from the sea."

After leaving the seer, Melicertes did some hard thinking. "Can I believe that pompous old charlatan? What did he say, after all? My death will come from the sea. What kind of prophecy is that? We're all pirate-kings in this part of the world. Our death usually comes from the sea, even as our wealth does."

27

So the king strode toward the stables, trying to reassure himself. But he wasn't able to. He couldn't shake off the memory of those empty sockets fixed on him, and the deep quiet voice saying, "You have devised your own death, Melicertes."

He entered the paddock and worked the horses for a while, but stopped sooner than was his custom. They were off their feed, sluggish and irritable. One stallion actually snapped at him. He did not return to the palace. He walked along the chariot course, trying to recall his greatest triumphs. But they would not come. All he saw were the puckered red sockets staring at him, the bony hand, gesturing.

"He couldn't have meant that I
was to perish . . . in a tidal wave."

"Let me approach this another way," he told himself. "Let me examine the prophecy as if it contained some truth. My death will come from the sea. He couldn't have meant that I was to perish in some ordinary sea battle or drown in a tidal wave. He must have meant something special. Some doom springing from one of my own actions. Accursed old wizard! I should have drawn my dagger and finished him off then and there. Why didn't I? Actually, it's tricky, killing oracles. Some of them claim to enjoy the special patronage of the gods."

Then, suddenly, Melicertes was swept by the feeling that he had thought this same thought before—that he had decided to kill someone and had been stopped by the same fear of divine reprisal.

"Yes!" he cried. "I remember! It was when I was about to throw that babe off the cliff after his stubborn mother—but I held back because she had said he was the son of a god. Poseidon's son! That's it! Of course . . . that brat that I took into my home and raised as my own, the one they call Bellerophon, is sea-spawned; it is he who plans my death. *He* is the death from the sea. Well, I'll turn that prophecy upside down. I'll be his death before he's mine."

And the king stumped off to find Bellerophon.

7

The Mad King

ellerophon saw him approaching. The man's lips were writhing in a horrible way, and he realized that the king was trying to smile. The youth had had little acquaintance with fear. But now he felt something strange clutching at his windpipe. He knew that he was in mortal danger. Suspicion hardened to certainty as the smirking king came closer and dropped a heavy hand on his shoulder.

"Greetings, young fellow," said Melicertes.

"Greetings, majesty."

"We haven't had much conversation together, you and I. Royal business presses hard, you know. And I may have been neglecting my household a bit. But now I intend to pay more attention to my sons and heirs. Tell me something about yourself, lad—your likes and dislikes, your hopes and disappointments."

"It's very good of you, sir," stammered Bellerophon, "to take such an interest."

"Well, I'm a family man at heart. And there's something about you that attracts my special attention. Tell me, do you like horses?"

"No, your majesty, I do not. I'm fond of animals in general, but not of horses."

"Prepare to pit your chariot against mine."

"I see. . . . Is it because of the unusual reputation my stock has gained?"

"Frankly, sire, I'm afraid of them. We all are."

"I'm sorry to hear that. For I have planned a series of chariot races, pitting me against each of my sons, beginning with you."

"With me?" asked Bellerophon.

"I have to start somewhere, and I have decided to start with the youngest, who happens to be you."

"Well . . . I'm honored. But . . . "

"In my kingdom, you see, the eldest son does not automatically inherit the throne. I intend to choose my own successor. To do it fairly I mean to test the mettle of my heirs one by one, starting, as I say, with you."

"But sire, what kind of race could I put up? I'd be too frightened to harness those great savage beasts, let alone drive them."

"My boy," said Melicertes, "let me give you a little advice. The thing most to be feared in Corinth is displeasing the king. And it is my pleasure now, Bellerophon, to ask you to pick a team of horses out of my stock, and prepare to pit your chariot against mine. The race shall take place seven days hence, when the sun reaches midpoint between noon and dusk. Do you understand?"

"I understand. I shall do as you ask. But I can't promise you an interesting race."

"Just be there, and ready. I assure you I shall enjoy myself."

"Thank you for the opportunity to demonstrate my mettle," said Bellerophon.

"Thank me after the race," said the king.

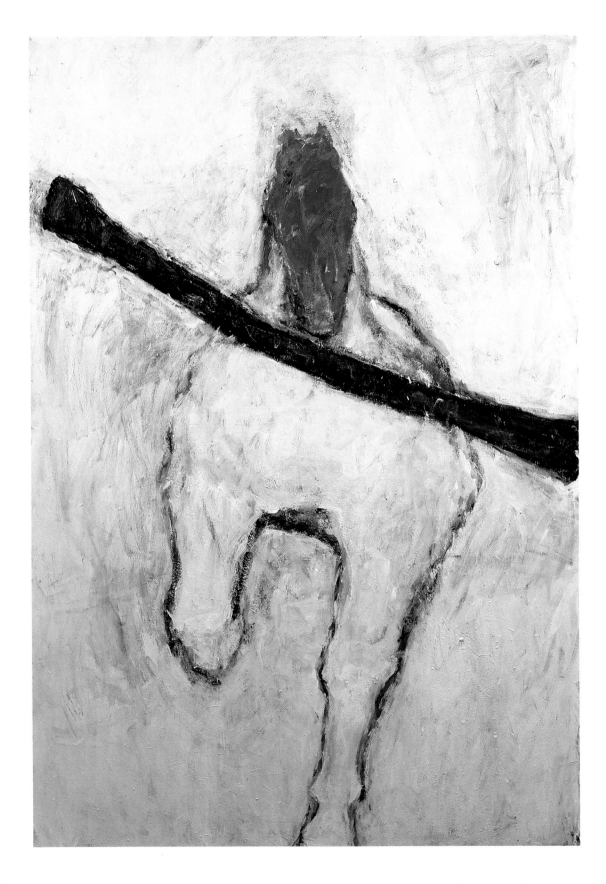

8

A Gathering Doom

lmost dusk, and the day was dying bloodily. The huge disk of the sun dipped into the sea, coloring it with drowned fires—crimson, fading to pink, turning to purple and gold. Bellerophon wandered along the beach, trying to think of a way to survive the king's sudden attention.

"Through the years, I have become fairly familiar with the methods used by our murderous ruler," he mused. "Now if I can only guess which one he means to use on me I may have a chance of staying alive. Let's see, what's the first victim I remember? The king of Arcadia, who protested being fouled in a race; why he was simply shot from ambush by one of the royal archers. That's one way he might get rid of me. If so, though, why would Melicertes be proposing all this rigmarole of a chariot race? No, he probably won't call on his archers. After all, for a prince of Corinth to be killed by an arrow shot from ambush might give the general public ideas about how to get rid of royalty. I should think he would want my death to appear an accident. And, of course, racing a chariot against him is a classic way for accidents to happen.

The day was dying bloodily.

"There was the king of Thessaly, for example, whose wheel rolled off in mid-course, hurling him from his chariot and breaking his neck. If anyone suspected that Melicertes had arranged for an axle pin to be removed before the race . . . well, such suspicions are not voiced in Corinth. I'll make sure to examine my wheels very carefully before the race begins.

"Perhaps he plans a simpler way, though. For the horses to turn on me when I try to harness them. For my unfortunate demise to occur before the race is even underway. Yes, he may well choose that method. For, thanks to my mother's wise ghost, I have kept my horsemanship a secret; the king, despite all his spies, knows nothing of it.

"But no! Something tells me it would be fatal to expect him to do the obvious. He may not know about me and the horses, but he has a brute cunning that has made him the most successful, most lethal tyrant of his time. I sense that he will try some other way. But what way? I feel a doom gathering about me, and I can't seem to think my way out."

Bellerophon kept pacing the water's edge, mulling things over. "Perhaps," he said to himself, "I'm doing too much thinking. This can be fatal. Here I stroll under a kindling sky, admiring the changing colors of the sea, trying to guess which unexpected thing the king plans for me when I should be preparing some unexpected things myself. That's always the key to victory—to surprise the enemy, to move before he does. It's more my style, anyway." And before he could think better of it, Bellerophon ran off to find the king.

9

Hooves of Death

e found the king in his throne room, affixing a massive ruby to the end of his ivory scepter. Melicertes looked up as the youth approached and watched him out of eyes as cold and black as a lizard's.

"What a magnificent stone," murmured Bellerophon.

"It's just like the one used by Minos," said the king. "He was an early ruler of Crete, and the monarch I most admire. The knob of his scepter was a blood-red ruby so that he might bash in the skull of whoever displeased him without staining the gem."

"Excuse me for interrupting your statesmanlike labors, your majesty, but something has been weighing on my conscience."

"Conscience?" said Melicertes. "That's a luxury no king can afford. If you hope to rule, my boy, you had better get rid of yours."

"Thank you for your good counsel," said Bellerophon. "You are as wise as you are generous. But what has been bothering me is that in the matter of this chariot race, you are being unfair to yourself."

"Unfair to myself? That doesn't sound like me. What do you mean?"

"Well, you see, you are of—imposing physique. You must outweigh me by fifty pounds, sixty perhaps. That will give my horses less to pull, of course, and put you at a disadvantage in the race."

The king studied the lad silently. Finally he spoke: "You're a curious chap. How is it you are concerned about some weight advantage instead of worrying about being eaten by my horses? Everyone fears them; don't you?"

Bellerophon hesitated a moment, then said: "I do fear them, but I don't think they'll eat me. I'm of too salty a flavor."

"What do you mean too salty?" cried the king.

"I am sea-spawned, your majesty. My father is Poseidon."

"Who told you that?" roared the king. "I've ordered that no one tell you that."

"No one did," said Bellerophon. "No one alive, that is. The ghost of my mother appeared to me and informed me of the circumstances of my birth."

"She did, did she? And did she inform you of the circumstances of her death?"

"No, sir, she did not."

"Did she tell you she knew me?"

"I believe she mentioned that you had honored her with your friendship before her departure."

Bellerophon watched the king closely. He balanced himself on the balls of his feet. His hand, hidden by his tunic, crept toward his dagger. For envenomed recognition was humming between them now. Hatred, like love, was enabling them to read each other's minds.

"He knows that I know he killed my mother," thought Bellerophon. "What will he do now—strike me with that scepter or take me to the stables and turn the horses on me?"

*Crossing the courtyard under a great
brass gong of a moon, Bellerophon felt
the king's hand close . . . with brutal force.*

He saw the king's knuckles whiten as he clutched the scepter, and his own fingers found the hilt of his dagger. He breathed a silent prayer: "Poseidon, father, help me now."

Then Bellerophon spoke aloud, very quickly, almost gabbling. "Since I am no natural son of yours, I have no claim upon the throne, and there is no reason for you to consider me a candidate for kingship—therefore no reason to test my mettle. We may as well call off the race, don't you think?"

"No," said the king. "That's not what I think, not at all. Actually I'm more eager for the race than ever. In fact, we shall go to the stables right now, you and I, and you will choose your horses. It's not too early to make their acquaintance."

More than ever inspired by hatred, seeing even more clearly now into the foul cave of the king's mind, Bellerophon read the scene that was gathering there—man and youth approaching the stalls where the great beasts stood, the king holding a torch, making the shadows dance, his big hand shooting out and striking the lad between the shoulders, shoving him forward so that he stumbled and fell, as the horses raged out of their stalls, eyes rolling, foam flying, teeth glistening.

"You want us to go to the horses now, at night?" he asked, trying to make his voice tremble.

"Right now," said the king. "Immediately."

"But won't they be more irritable, being awakened from sleep? More likely to attack someone they don't know?"

"What do you care? You're too salty, you say. They won't eat you."

"Well," said Bellerophon, "they don't have to accept me just because they find me inedible. They can still batter me to death with their hooves."

"But I'll be with you, my boy, introducing you to them. Recommending you to their special consideration. I assure you, they'll know you well before you leave."

Crossing the courtyard under a great brass gong of a moon, Bellerophon felt the king's hand close on his upper arm with brutal force.

"Does he mean to kill me now?" thought the lad. "Bash out my brains with that scepter before we get to the stables? Can I reach my dagger before he strikes?"

But the king did not raise his scepter. He simply marched the slender lad toward the stables. There, it all became what Bellerophon had seen before, pictured in the king's mind: the massive double doors swinging open, the huge rustling stable, the fragrance of horses, hulking man and slender youth standing silently, staring into the darkness. The only difference was that the king held no torch. Hot yellow moonlight poured through the doors, making the shadows dance.

There, it all became what Bellerophon had
seen before, pictured in the king's mind:
the massive doors . . . the fragrance of horses.

Bellerophon knew what would happen next. He let his muscles go loose—let himself slip into a kind of alert drowse that cut off his ordinary responses and tuned him, every pore and fiber, to the pent wildness of *Horse*. He felt the king's hand between his shoulder blades, felt himself being pushed violently.

*The last sight the king saw was
what so many of his victims had seen.*

He went with it, and did not stumble. But stood silently as a pair of stallions burst out of their stalls, rearing, pawing the air with their forehooves, eyes rolling, teeth gleaming.

The king smiled as the great horses obscured the boy. He waited for them to strike down with their forehooves, waited to hear Bellerophon scream.

What he heard was his own strangled voice, gasping "No!"

For the horses had come down gently. Their muzzles nudged the boy's shoulders. They nuzzled him, whickering softly.

The king let out a piercing scream. For Bellerophon was pointing at him, and the horses had turned and were glaring with utter ferocity—with that bestial blankness as if he were some poor condemned wretch instead of himself, Melicertes, their master and master of Corinth, most feared of all kings.

The last sight the king saw was what so many of his victims had seen—huge teeth, glaring eyes, flying spittle, hooves like hatchets falling.

Melicertes, realizing how he had been tricked into devising his own death, felt his proud heart burst with vexation, saving him a few moments of final agony as the stallions trampled him to a pulp on the floor of the royal stable.

10

Anteia

fter contriving the death of the king, Bellerophon found himself very weary and returned to his chambers to sleep. But he was awakened before dawn by the ghost of his mother who whispered certain instructions.

She departed, but sleep had fled. Bellerophon rushed back to the stables, saddled his favorite horse, and galloped eastward. When he reached the palace at Tiryns, he was met by a glittering official who told him coldly that the king was out hunting and the queen was in the garden, and that neither, in any case, was in the habit of receiving casual visitors.

"I'm not casual, I'm kin," said Bellerophon. "And I suggest that you trundle your portly self out to the garden and inform the queen that her cousin, a prince of Corinth, seeks the honor of her acquaintance."

Now, as Chief Steward, this official considered himself a particularly important personage. He drew himself up as tall as he could, swelling like a frog, preparing to summon the royal guard. But perhaps he would expel the fellow himself; he was a slender lad, and didn't seem capable of much resistance.

As he looked into the keen young face, however, he detected a frigid gleam in those gray eyes, and felt an icy sliver of fear lodge in his gut. "After all," he thought to himself, "if the lad is some sort of relative, perhaps I'd better show him a little courtesy."

Aloud, he said, "Follow me, prince. I'll lead you to her majesty."

What he saw was a wand of a girl, with petal skin and enormous green eyes.

He strutted down a winding path, leading Bellerophon through a fringe of trees and onto another path that opened into a flower garden.

"Your majesty," he boomed, "Bellerophon, prince of Corinth!"

He stepped back, and vanished.

Bellerophon saw no one. The massed roses distilled the light, half blinding him. A heavy fragrance enveloped him, making him half drunk. He stood in a pink mist, feeling himself fill with delight. A figure swam out of the roses and stood before him. He shook his head, dazed. The title 'queen' had made him picture an elderly, imposing lady. But what he saw was a wand of a girl, with petal skin and enormous green eyes.

Bellerophon tried to say something but couldn't. He sank to one knee, took her hand, and touched his lips to the palm—and understood how a bee felt burying itself into the heart of a rose. He did not let go her hand, nor did she pull it away, but pulled him to his feet.

"You're a cousin, you say—from Corinth?"

"Yes, ma'am."

"Have you come as an ambassador, bearing messages from your father to my husband?"

"Melicertes will send no more messages, my lady. He got himself killed by his horses."

"Who is king, then?" asked the girl.

"It is undecided. There's a struggle going on for the throne. He had lots of sons, you see, and most of them are ambitious."

"Aren't you?"

"Not in the same way. Besides, I have no claim to the crown. Melicertes wasn't my real father; I was adopted."

"That wouldn't stop you from being ambitious. You have the look about you of a young man who might jump at an empty throne."

"Do I? I guess that's what my brothers think too. That's why Corinth's unhealthy for me right now, and that's why I'm here."

"Oh really?" said the girl. "I thought, perhaps, you were attracted to Tiryns by reports of my beauty."

"Well, you are very beautiful, of course," said Bellerophon, "but I didn't hear about it there."

The queen laughed.

"Oh, you're just joking," said Bellerophon. "Well, it was my mother who told me to come. I didn't want to leave Corinth, even though several brothers were conspiring to kill me, but my mother insisted. 'Go to Tiryns,' she said. 'You have cousins there.'"

"Did she not mention my name?" asked the queen.

"My mother's dead, actually. It's her ghost who visits me."

"Often?"

"Just when I'm in danger of some kind. She doesn't stay long—just appears and says 'do this, do that.' She wouldn't have known about you, maybe, because you would have been only a child when she died. You look very young to be married and a queen.''

"Well, you've come to the right place, my dear, sweet, new cousin. And the queen of Tiryns hereby officially welcomes you.''

She smiled mischievously, lightly kissed his lips, and glided back into the roses. He followed. He took the pruning knife from her hand, and bent to the flowers.

"Careful," she murmured. "They have thorns."

Returning from the hunt, Proetus, king of Tiryns, sent for his wife, and was informed that she was not in her chambers but in the garden, conversing with a young stranger. Instructing the captain of the royal guard to follow him at a distance, the king hurried to the garden.

Bellerophon and Anteia were standing amongst the roses, staring at each other. He was trying to think of something to say; she waited, smiling. Past the shining fall of her hair, the lad saw someone enter the garden—a man, tall and thin, with a face like a meat cleaver. He was in hunting clothes and wore no crown, but Bellerophon, raised in the court of a tyrant, knew immediately that here was another who demanded complete and instant obedience. Coming toward them in the green garments of the chase, the king looked like a weed, the kind that strangles roses. He came closer and stood over them, saying nothing, glaring from one face to the other.

"Greetings, my lord," said Anteia. "May I present to you our cousin, Bellerophon, prince of Corinth."

The king stood motionless for a moment, staring at the young man. Then he spoke in a dust-dry voice. "Are you here on official embassy, young sir? Do you bear messages from Melicertes?"

"No, your majesty, I bear no message."

"But he brings important news!" cried Anteia. "Melicertes is dead, and there is strife in Corinth as his many sons contend for the throne."

"That information has already reached me through other channels," said the king. "Is that what brings you here, prince—to ask me to support your claim to the throne?"

"No, sir," said Bellerophon. "I make no such claim."

"Then why, may I ask, have you decided to honor us with your presence? A sudden impulse of kinship?"

"He's just passing through, my lord," said Anteia. "He's on his way to Lycia."

Now, Bellerophon, of course, had no such intention. He barely knew where Lycia was. But he realized that the girl was saying the first thing that came to her mind.

"Lycia, eh?" said Proetus. "To visit my esteemed father-in-law? He's not doing much entertaining these days. Some undiscriminating monster seems to find the Lycians very appetizing. This lady's father, the king of that land, is quite frantic with worry. He has been hoping, for some reason, that the gods will send a hero to slay the beast, but he's beginning to realize that the gods are forgetful, and that monsters are more plentiful than heroes."

Bellerophon and Anteia were standing amongst the roses, staring at each other.

Bellerophon turned to the girl. "Have you seen this creature?"

"It has a name," said Anteia. "It's called the Chimaera. Those who see it at close range are devoured. Those who glimpse it from afar and manage to escape are too frightened to see straight, and their descriptions vary. But we do know that it's gigantic, it flies, it spits fire—and eats everything in sight."

"Perhaps you'll see for yourself when you get there," said the king.

"Possibly," said Bellerophon, who thought to himself: "This weasel-faced bully is worse than Melicertes. I am much inclined to strike him down where he stands and run away with his wife. But that hulking brute of a guard stands too close, and the rest of his troop is undoubtedly hiding in the underbrush. They'd be upon me before I could draw my sword."

Aloud, he said: "Farewell, gracious queen. Do you have any message for your father?"

"Yes!" she cried. "Tell him I love him! Tell him not to despair. A hero will come one day and slay the Chimaera. I know he will."

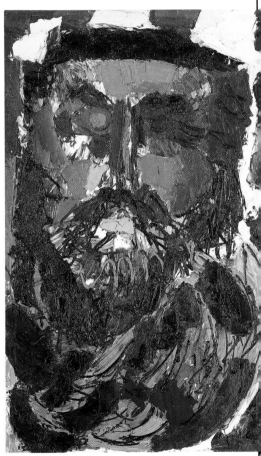

The king stood motionless for a moment, staring at the young man.

She burst into tears and ran out of sight behind the roses.

"Cousin," said Proetus. "I think you had better be on your way without any more ceremony. I don't like young men speaking to my wife, cousin or not. And my captain of the guard over there, that huge fellow standing in the shade of the tree, is quick to read my wish, even that which remains unspoken. His method is simple, bless him, a bowstring about the neck of the offender, inducing acute strangulation—and behold! Whoever has displeased me will do so no more. You wouldn't want to fall into the hands of such a fellow, would you?"

"I thank you for your hospitality," said Bellerophon, and departed.

11

The Hunt Begins

When Bellerophon had left Corinth, he had taken one of the horses that had killed the king, a huge gray stallion. He named it Sea Mist, and it became more than a mount to him. The horse was a fierce guardian, a loyal companion. During the long ride Bellerophon had fallen into the habit of speaking his thoughts to it.

Now, riding the great gray stallion out of Tiryns toward Lycia, Bellerophon suddenly wheeled the horse about and began to ride back. Then he stopped, and sat there on the horse's back, torn by indecision.

"I must go back and fetch her!" he cried. "No weedy tyrant will stop me, nor all his murderous bodyguard. Yes, we must return immediately. . . . But how do I know that she wants me to? A few soft words, a smile, a cousinly kiss—are they enough to build on? Why, she's the most beautiful girl in the world, and married to a very rich, very powerful king; could she really prefer me? Why do I think so? I do, but I'm not sure. When I asked if she had any message for her father, she cried, 'Tell him I love him!' and her throbbing voice seemed to say, 'Not only him, but

Bellerophon leaped onto the stallion's
back . . . and they galloped away.

you too.' Could she have meant that? Or did I hear what I wanted to hear? She has reason to be concerned about her father, of course, deviled as he is by that Chimaera, waiting for a hero that does not come."

Bellerophon had dismounted and was leaning against the horse. He cried out suddenly, startling the animal. Then he clasped its great neck, exclaiming, "That's it! Yes! Why didn't I think of it before? I'll go and kill the monster that's been tormenting her father. We'll start right now. We won't even stop at the royal palace in Lycia, but go to the hills immediately, and begin our Chimaera hunt. She'll have to love me if I kill it, won't she? Surely she will. And you'll enjoy the hunt, won't you, Sea Mist? You haven't had much action lately.''

He leaped onto the stallion's back, drummed his heels, and they galloped away.

12

Dangerous Passage

Last reports had placed the Chimaera among the Lycian hills, and it was there that Bellerophon rode. The track was easy to follow; the monster had left terrible traces. From village to devastated village, Bellerophon stalked the monster. Sometimes he came so close that houses were still burning when he arrived and the kill was so fresh that vultures had not yet come to strip the bones.

Eagerly, he searched the sky for smoke plumes. Sometimes, he thought he saw gray coils winding up in the sky, and his heart would leap, but it was only the mist or a wisp of cloud. Once, he was sure that he saw the monster as a speck on the horizon growing larger and larger. He drew his sword and shouted a battle cry. But it was only an eagle hunting goats.

"I don't understand it," he said to the horse. "Everyone else tries to avoid the monster, and dies in the process, while I, who want so desperately to find it, can't even catch a glimpse of the damned thing. Perhaps some god is playing games with me."

The next village Bellerophon came to had not yet been destroyed. When he questioned the villagers, he found them unwilling to answer, as if they feared that any mention of the Chimaera might make it appear. Finally, a child told him that he had seen the beast flying high, in the direction of the sea.

"Back to the coast, then!" cried Bellerophon. And the horse went into its tireless swinging trot.

On the way, Bellerophon devised a plan, which he confided to the horse. "I've heard that the Chimaera attacks fishing fleets, for then it can eat the catch as well as those who do the catching. What I shall do is leave you on shore, swim out to one of the boats, climb aboard, and wait for the monster to attack."

When the youth had left Corinth, he had also taken the dead king's sword, a magnificent weapon, with a blade so sharp it could cut a floating feather in two. Its hand guard was made

Beach and piers were empty.

of beaten copper and its hilt was wrapped in tough, pliant calf's hide, stitched with gold wire. "I must have it," Bellerophon had said to himself, standing over his fallen foe. "I killed an enemy who was trying to kill me, and by the rules of battle I am entitled to his weapon. It's not theft, it's legitimate loot."

But this priceless sword was to plunge Bellerophon into an adventure that threatened to end his career before he encountered the Chimaera.

Riding along, he could smell a salt wind now, and glimpsed the sea like a tilted tin plate, reflecting the sunlight. He had decided not to ride all the way to the shore, afraid that the faithful horse might follow him into the water when he tried to swim out to the fishing vessels.

He stopped, dismounted, and instructed Sea Mist to roam the meadows and wait for him until he should return. The stallion laid back its ears, nudged him with its head, and whickered plaintively. But the lad said, "You can't come. Wait for me here." He set off on foot, trying to shut his ears to the lonely, trumpeting cry the horse sent after him.

The piers were empty. A large school of mullet had been sighted and the entire fleet had been put out to sea. They had sailed a good distance; Bellerophon saw only smudges on the horizon. He knew that the boats would not have bunched themselves, but would be strung out for miles, for fishermen of the same village gave one another generous room to cast their nets.

The shore was rocky here. Bellerophon began searching for a break in the boulder line where he might enter the water and begin his long swim. He heard someone shouting, and turned.

A huge, burly man was clambering over the rocks toward him. He was bearded and swarthy, with a look of subdued ferocity, but he spoke courteously: "Good day, stranger. You are a stranger, are you not?"

"I am," said Bellerophon. "My home is Corinth."

"I saw that you were gazing out to sea as if trying to identify some vessel out there. I know most of the folk hereabout. Is there someone special you're looking for?"

"No, sir," replied Bellerophon. "But I mean to join a crew. My intention is to swim out and board one of the fishing boats."

"You won't make it," said the man. "There are sharks in these waters; they tend to cluster around fishing boats when the catch is good."

"Thank you, sir. I appreciate your advice. Nevertheless, I mean to get out there, sharks or not."

"I can save you a long dangerous swim," said the stranger. "I was just about to join the fleet myself. My ship's waiting in the next cove. I'll be glad to give you passage."

"You're very kind. What is your fee?"

"No fee at all," said the man. "We here on this coast have a reputation for hospitality."

The man led Bellerophon along the rocky shore to a cove where a black vessel lay moored. The crew was as savage looking as the captain, but said nothing as Bellerophon boarded. He noticed that the ship carried no nets, but he forgot all about that in the excitement of setting sail.

The ship was fast. It scudded before the wind. Bellerophon searched the sky as they sailed, hoping to spot the Chimaera. He did not realize that there were other dangerous creatures prowling much closer. For fishing was not the sole occupation of the coast dwellers. Many of them found piracy more profitable. And the crew of this particular vessel happened to be the most viciously successful pirates in those waters.

Blinded to everything else by his desire to find the Chimaera, the lad did not realize his peril until a heavy hand clamped his shoulder and swung him around. It was the captain. His other hand held an ax.

"Farewell, stranger," he said.

"Why farewell?" stammered Bellerophon.

"You are about to leave us, young sir. A final journey, in fact."

"But why?"

"Because you're too foolish to live."

"What have I done that is so foolish?"

"You have come among us alone, wearing a treasure at your belt. Very unwise."

"But why?"

"Because we're pirates, of course. Pirates take what they want and throw the rest away."

"You mean you want my sword?"

"Exactly. Indeed, I have considered it *my* sword ever since I first laid eyes on it. And the time has come to take possession."

"But why must you kill me?" asked Bellerophon. "Just take the thing and let me go."

"I can understand your point of view," said the pirate. "But it just doesn't work that way. We don't like to leave witnesses; it's not our policy. However, I can assure you, you'll feel no pain. I'm a skilled axman, and this blade will shear through your neck so swiftly that you won't feel a thing until you're reunited with your head down in Hades."

"I appreciate your compassion," said the youth. "Please . . . take my sword." Bellerophon drew it from its sheath, and, with a lightning flexion of his arm, whisked the blade through

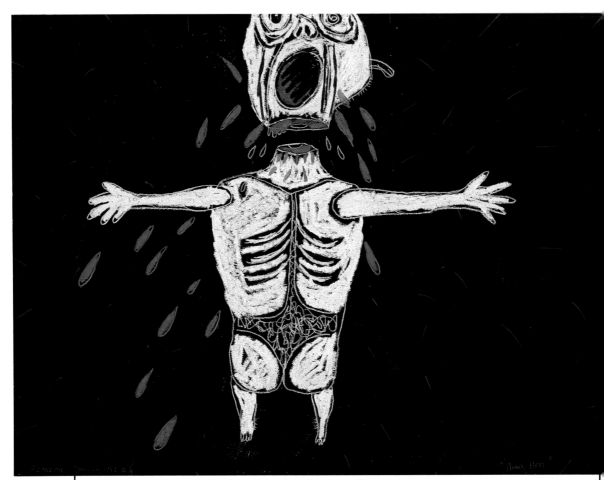

With a lightning flexion of his
arm, Bellerophon whisked the
blade through the pirate's neck.

the pirate's thick neck like a cook cutting a celery stalk. The body fell to the deck, spouting blood. The head rolled into the scuppers.

"You'll be reunited with it in Hades!" shouted Bellerophon, and jumped overboard as the other pirates rushed at him.

Remembering the sharks, he swam under the ship and clung to its keel—a position that tended to discourage sharks, who need space above them to turn and strike. He hung on to the keel, pondering what to do. He had no fear of drowning. As a son of Poseidon, he could breathe underwater. But his wet clothes clung to him, and after a while he began to feel cold. "No use," he thought. "I'll have to swim back to shore. If there are any sharks about, I'll give them some distraction."

Drawing his sword underwater, he stabbed it through the planking of the ship, stabbed again and again, until he knew it was taking on a weight of water. He swam out from under the sinking vessel, cleaving the water as swiftly as a seal, for he didn't know how long the drowning pirates would occupy the sharks. He heard men screaming as he headed toward shore, and swam faster than ever.

13

The Ghost Returns

pon reaching shore, Bellerophon immediately struck inland, and did not stop until he came to the meadow where he had left Sea Mist. He heard a rushing, a drumming of hooves; the stallion's eyes were pits of yellow light as it came thundering across the field to greet the lad.

"I'll tell you all about it in the morning," Bellerophon said to the horse. "But let's sleep now. I'm weary."

Bellerophon awoke while it was still dark. He heard her voice before he saw her. The moon was half veiled by clouds, and the horse, bulking in the weak moonlight, looked like a bank of fog. She drifted closer as the moon swam clear, and Bellerophon was able to make out a faint shape.

"Welcome, mother," he said. "If ever I required good counsel, I do so now."

"That is why I have come to you, my son."

"I'm heartsick and weary, mother. I'm helpless against the Chimaera. Nothing I do alters the course of the beast. He's here, there, and everywhere, killing, destroying, and I can't even find him."

"I'm not aware that I ever counseled you to go monster hunting."

*The horse, bulking in the weak
moonlight, looked like a bank of fog.*

"No, mother, that was my own idea."

"Are you sure you want to be a hero? It doesn't leave much room in life for other things, you know."

"It's not the title I'm after. I don't want the name; I want the deed. I have a special reason for wishing to kill the Chimaera."

"Hearken, son," said the ghost.

> To perform this deed
> you need a steed
> who's half your brother,
> son of your father,
> But not of your mother.

"Need a steed?" cried Bellerophon. "I have one, a marvellous one. He's over there. Isn't he a beauty?"

"Can he fly?"

"He runs like the wind. He seems to fly."

"Seeming is not enough. To kill a monster demands all kinds of hard realities. To vanquish this one, which flies better than any bird, you will need a horse that flies as swiftly."

"What kind of horse can do that?"

"One with wings."

"Is there such a creature?" asked Bellerophon.

"There is. A great white stallion with golden wings—and many other unusual attributes. He is of divine stock, having been sired by Poseidon upon one of his earlier brides, the snake-haired Medusa."

"She who was slain by the hero, Perseus?"

"The same. When Perseus cut off her head, two drops of blood fell to the ground. From one of them sprang the winged horse, Pegasus, whom, it is decreed, you must ride if you are to vanquish the Chimaera and claim Anteia."

"You know about her then."

"Of course. I know everything about you. It's the only knowledge that reaches me in Hades."

"But will Anteia have me if I slay the Chimaera?"

"Is it not this hope that has launched you on your perilous quest?" asked the ghost.

"Yes . . . yes it is. But sometimes I think that it's only my own fantasy. A wild dream."

"Wild dreams can become wilder realities. But only if you make them so."

"What shall I do, mother?"

"Seek the winged horse."

"Where?"

"On the slopes of Mount Helicon, in the land of Boeotia. Godspeed, my lovely boy."

14

The Winged Horse

raveling night and day, Bellerophon rode his great gray stallion out of Lycia back toward Boeotia. They reached Mount Helicon at mid-morning. It was a cloudless day; the hillside shimmered in a green haze. Searching the near slope, Bellerophon spotted a patch of whiteness, too large for sheep or goat. He rode uphill and saw gold flashing upon the whiteness. Coming closer, he gasped in wonder. A stallion of astounding beauty stood before him, snow-white and tall as a stag, with golden wings and mane, coral-red nostrils, and brass hooves.

"Pegasus!" he shouted. Dismounting, he ran toward the horse. The animal tossed its head and moved away. Bellerophon heard Sea Mist neighing in a tone he had never heard before. Turning, he saw the stallion's great eyes brimming with tears.

"No!" cried Bellerophon, running toward Sea Mist. But the horse whirled and galloped away, racing down the slope and out of sight before Bellerophon could reach him.

"He's jealous," thought the lad. "The sight of me going after that magnificent winged horse was more than he could bear. Well, I can't think about it now; I've got to catch Pegasus."

Bellerophon was starting uphill again when a little man popped out from behind a rock as if he had been hiding there. "Greetings!" he cried. "My name is Thallo. What's yours?"

"Bellerophon."

The little man limped toward him, and Bellerophon saw that both his legs were twisted. He waited, quivering with impatience. Finally, Bellerophon said: "I don't wish to seem discourteous, sir, but I'm in somewhat of a hurry."

"No one's in a hurry here," the little man replied. "Are you sure you're in the right place?"

"This is Mount Helicon, isn't it?" asked the lad.

"Mount Helicon, indeed, where the Muses dwell, and where Pegasus finds pasture. To these slopes unpublished poets flock. For they believe that a short ride on the winged horse will endow them with the talent they lack. I know—I was among the first to try that flight. Pegasus let me mount him, and with one beat of his golden wings soared above the top of that cedar tree. I would have been dizzy with fear had I not been consumed by ecstacy. For, as we rose and the earth tilted beneath us, verses began to sing in my head. Oh, they were magical lines, sparkling with wit, brimming with melody. And just as I was beginning to savor my own worth, the damned brute bucked me off. I fell a long way, shattering both legs when I hit the ground."

"And you've been here ever since?" asked Bellerophon.

"Certainly. I wasn't going to drag myself back to Thrace. They're a warlike breed there, splendid specimens every one, curse them. They didn't show much regard for me when I had two good legs: just imagine what chance I'd stand with them as a cripple. So, here I dwell, trying to recapture the verses I composed during my brief flight, and which were knocked out of my head when I fell."

"Is that all you do?"

"All? Did you say all?" groaned the little man. "It's a lifetime occupation, my dear sir. It leaves no room for anything else. Of course, I spend some time observing other would-be poets trying to ride Pegasus, deriving a bitter pleasure from seeing them fall as I did."

"Are they here too, all the others?"

"They are indeed. In that grove yonder you will find an encampment of gimpy versifiers. They cluster about a spring called Hippocrene, whose waters are said to possess healing powers, especially for those wounded in the service of the Muse. But I don't associate with them. I keep to myself, working on a great ballad, which I just began this year and which I wouldn't mind reciting to you if you can spare a few hours of utter attention."

"Thank you," replied Bellerophon, "but I can't. I'm on an urgent mission."

*"In that grove you will find an encampment
of gimpy versifiers. They cluster about a spring
whose waters are said to possess healing powers."*

"Urgent? What could be more urgent than this? You shall be the first to hear verses that will be sung four thousand years hence."

"I'm not much on poetry."

"Oh, these verses will change all that. They're not dreamy, moon-beamy stuff, but a story-song, full of violence and romance. Salted with reality. The story of Melicertes, king of Corinth, who was eaten by his own horses, all set in immortal quatrains."

"They didn't eat him," muttered Bellerophon.

"What did you say?"

"Melicertes's horses. They kicked him to death but didn't eat him."

"Please, my boy, I'm concerned with matters of meter and rhyme. I can't be bothered with facts that don't fit. How do you know so much about it, anyway?"

"I come from Corinth. And now I must be on my way. I appreciate your conversation, good sir, but I must bridle Pegasus and ride him to Lycia, where the Chimaera hunts."

"Ride Pegasus? So you too are a would-be poet? No wonder you don't want to hear anyone else's work."

"I want Pegasus, sir, to ride into battle with the Chimaera."

"Into battle? On that treacherous beast? You won't get past the top of the cedars."

"Watch me," said Bellerophon.

Pegasus was grazing on the slope somewhat above where the two men stood. Bellerophon moved toward the horse, calling softly, making the whickering sound that he used to call Sea Mist. Pegasus did not respond, did not raise his head. He was cropping grass and kept moving away as the young man approached.

Thallo had followed. "If you're really mad enough to want to ride him," he said, "stand on that spur of rock there. Hunch your shoulders, groan a little, tear your hair. He'll think you're a poet and come to you. There's nothing he enjoys more than lifting us toward the heavens, then bucking us off, damn him."

"Thanks," said Bellerophon.

The youth clambered onto the long spur of rock that jutted from the mountainside and overlooked the valley. He hunched his shoulders, groaned, and pulled his hair. He saw the great white stallion soaring toward him on golden wings.

Bellerophon leaped from the rock onto the horse's back. He had always loved the feeling that surged through him when astride a horse—as if the animal's wild power was entering him, turning him into something better than he was. But he had never felt anything as strong as the godlike force that was lifting him now into the blue, thin, intoxicating air.

Pegasus tilted his golden wings and, gull-like, caught a current of air, riding it up, up, past the cedar-tops. Bellerophon felt the weird power surging into his legs, turning bones into rods of iron, making them clamp the horse tighter. Pegasus bucked, but his rider was welded to him and holding fast.

The winged horse trumpeted furiously, and rolled over in the air. Bellerophon, hanging by his knees, saw the flowered slope spinning beneath him and shouted with glee as he spotted Thallo's amazed face lifted toward the sky.

Pegasus rolled over and over in the air. Bellerophon clung fast. With both hands, he stroked the horse that was trying to throw him, and kept talking to the enraged animal as earth

Pegasus bucked, but his rider was welded to him.

and sky kept changing places, blue spinning into green, and back again. But the youth clung as the horse whirled—never stopped stroking, crooning, using all the gentle, powerful skills he had learned breaking the wild horses of Corinth.

Suddenly, Pegasus stopped whirling, spread his wings, and coasted down. Bellerophon guided him by the pressure of his knees until the horse landed near Thallo and stood there, trembling. Bellerophon slid off and stroked the wonderful, strong neck—white and silky as Egyptian cloth.

Pegasus did not drop his head to his rider's shoulder and nuzzle him as other horses had done. The winged stallion was docile now, but he had not lost a shred of dignity. Bellerophon looked into his eyes. They were brilliant but blank; they were not to be read.

Bellerophon did not wish to fly to Lycia until the next day; he wanted to practice some aerial maneuvers with Pegasus before challenging the Chimaera. He also wished to practice his archery, which had grown rusty.

The young man camped on Helicon that night. There his mother came to him.

"Awake, my son," she called.

"Greetings, mother."

"Listen closely."

> When you leave this place
> go straight to Thrace.
> Between two peaks
> Man shall find
> what boy but seeks.
> At the last, I tell you this—
> to win the battle,
> make heads rattle.

Her voice stopped.

"No, stay!" he cried. But she had gone. Bellerophon felt confused; he had not understood her completely. She had told him that he would find the Chimaera in Thrace; that he knew. But he couldn't figure out the last couplet.

"She's sometimes mystifying, but never wrong," he said to himself. "So I'd better find out what I can about Thrace."

He went to where Thallo was sleeping nearby, curled like a fetus. He knelt and shook him gently. "What? Who? . . ." groaned the little man. He sat bolt upright. "It's you! You've changed your mind! You want to hear my ballad after all. Very well. I know it by heart."

"No, no," said Bellerophon. "No ballad. I want to hear about Thrace. You come from there, you say."

"Is that why you woke me?"

"Not because of an idle interest in geography, good Thallo. It's something much more important. My mother's ghost came to me tonight and told me that I would find the Chimaera in Thrace, so I go there in the morning."

"Ghosts, monsters. You give me an idea for a short tale to frighten children with. Just wait while I put together a few verses."

"Later, Thallo, please. This may be a matter of life and death. Tell me about Thrace."

"Well, it's not unlike Boeotia. Much larger; its plains are wider, its mountains higher. And, of course, it's much colder in winter. Really cold in the highlands. Sometimes the mountain passes are choked with snow."

"What's that?"

"You've never seen snow?"

"I don't know what it is—how do I know whether I've seen it?"

"It's a blossoming of frost," said Thallo. "The freezing sky drops slow white flowers that cling to mountain slopes and trees and pile up on the ground. In a hard season snow fills the passes

*"In a hard season snow fills the
passes so no one can get through."*

so no one can get through. That's why Thrace's neighbors feel
safe from attack in winter."

"It's winter now; I guess I'll see the snow, then," said
Bellerophon.

"Remember this, if you fly through a narrow pass, be careful not to make a loud noise. It can start an avalanche."

"What's that?"

"Snow, startled by noise, can come sliding down the mountain, growing larger and larger, tearing out pieces of mountain
and carrying them along, until finally tons of snow and rock are
falling, burying everything below."

"I'll be careful," said Bellerophon. "By the way, my mother mentioned something that I didn't understand. Perhaps you can. Something about a rattle."

"I don't know what she could have meant," said Thallo. "The only special rattles I know of are those used by marsh dwellers to protect themselves against the spear birds. These terrible creatures are larger than eagles and have beaks like spears; hence their name. They settle upon the marsh in great numbers, and the folk there string together old pots and helmets and odd bits of metal that they shake, making a dreadful clamor. This alone makes the birds fly away. I don't know how it might help you, though."

"Again, my thanks, good Thallo. I'll let you go back to sleep now. But I promise this: If I survive my encounter with the Chimaera, I shall return one day. I can give you some details about Corinth, and its mad king, and his man-eating horses, that may help you enrich your ballad."

"And will you tell about vanquishing the Chimaera?"

"Unless he vanquishes me," said Bellerophon.

15

The Chimaera

Bellerophon finally caught sight of the Chimaera as he was flying over a barren reach of ground—the last of the great Thracian plains before the highlands began. All he saw was a far glimpse of the monster vanishing in the distance. But it was unmistakable. And what it had left behind was sheer carnage. Apparently, it had caught a troop of warriors in the open field and dived upon them like a hawk striking a flock of doves. It had killed them all and eaten them out of their armor as foxes flip turtles to eat them out of their shells.

Looking down, feeling himself grow dizzy with horror, Bellerophon saw breastplates, greaves, and helmets scattered about among the bones that wore only bloody tatters of flesh. Vultures coasted down to strip the corpses.

Pegasus needed no urging. He seemed to share Bellerophon's thoughts. Like a hound after a deer, he fastened on the scent of the Chimaera, and clove the air toward where the monster had disappeared.

"Did it see us?" the young man asked himself. "Is it trying to flee? Will it turn and fight? Father, Poseidon, make it turn!"

No sooner had he uttered this prayer, than he regretted it. For it was answered. There, hanging before him, was a grinning lion larger than an elephant—sulfur yellow, snarling, with claws poised. A winged lion with the body of a goat, but, most horrible, the tail of a serpent. When the beast curled its tail, a serpent's head appeared beside the lion head, both glaring at the tiny foolish midget of a mortal who dared to mount a horsefly and come monster hunting.

Pegasus had stopped in the air, and floated, facing the Chimaera. Bellerophon unslung his bow, notched an arrow, and let it fly, aiming at the beast's one vulnerable spot—the eye. The lion's jaws opened as if it were about to roar, but what issued from its mouth was flame, burning the arrow to a cinder as it flew through the air. Then, slowly, as if savoring its enemy's fear, the Chimaera soared toward Bellerophon.

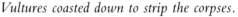

Vultures coasted down to strip the corpses.

Obeying his rider's thoughts, Pegasus immediately dived toward the mountainside and dipped low over a pine tree freighted with snow, allowing Bellerophon to break off an armful of wet green boughs. Pegasus climbed again, soaring swiftly until he was directly above the monster, and Bellerophon dropped the compacted bundle of branches in front of the beast. When it spat flame again, it was enveloped in dense black smoke as the green branches burned.

While the Chimaera groped blindly through the smoke, Bellerophon fled—not back toward the plains where he knew he'd be visible, but northward where mountains loomed, because he thought that, winding among crags, he might be able to hide from his pursuer. His pursuer . . . he was no longer hunting but being hunted. Bellerophon heard great leathery wings beating the air. He knew Pegasus could fly faster than the Chimaera, but he wasn't sure about the winged horse's endurance. At least for the moment, he could outrace the monster.

It grew colder as they flew. They were still angling upward. Snowy peaks towered above them. Bellerophon was searching for a cleft in the mountains, one too narrow for the Chimaera to follow him.

His mother's voice crooned in his head:

> Between two peaks
> Man shall find
> what boy but seeks.

Man, he was no man; he was a puling coward. As a boy he had been brave, had mastered savage horses, had challenged an even more savage king. Where had that courage gone? Could one sight of the grinning lion freeze his marrow, turn his heart to pulp?

He was seized by such a spasm of disgust that he was tempted to let himself slip off the horse's back and plunge to his death on the rocks below.

"But if I'm going to smash myself in a shameful fall," he thought, "I might as well imitate manhood by dying in the monster's jaws."

With that thought, he turned Pegasus around. Like a golden arrow, Pegasus flew back toward the Chimaera. Bellerophon bent low, shielding his face in the horse's mane, for the wind was blowing cold.

But he was hatching a plan as they flew, and again Pegasus understood. He slanted upward again, soaring so high that the air was almost too thin to breathe. Bellerophon gasped for breath. He felt the horse go into a dive. Looking back, he saw that they had passed over the Chimaera. As he watched, the monster turned and flew toward them.

Now they were nearing the plain where the dead warriors lay. He saw the foul litter on the ground, heard a rush of other wings as vultures rose from their feast.

As soon as Pegasus touched ground, Bellerophon was off the horse's back and running over the field. From corpse to corpse he ran, plucking helmets off skulls, tearing bloody tunics into rags, tying the rags together and stringing the helmets from them. When he had as many as he could carry, he mounted Pegasus again. The horse spread his wings and climbed into the air—just in time, for the Chimaera was almost upon them. A tongue of flame licked the air about them. Bellerophon felt the back of his neck scorching, smelled burning hair, and saw that the tip of Pegasus's golden tail was on fire. But the horse calmly swished his tail, putting out the blaze.

They climbed swiftly again, heading back toward the mountains. But they were going more slowly, for now they wished the monster to follow—not close enough to singe them with its flaming breath, but close enough to keep them in sight. They were among the mountains again, taking the exact path they had taken before. Bellerophon turned and saw the lion's head, saw the lashing serpent tail as the beast curved in the air, making a tight turn around a crag.

Pegasus had stopped in the air, and floated, facing the Chimaera.

They were high enough now. The mountain slopes were packed with snow. Neither rock nor tree could be seen. Then Bellerophon found what he was looking for—a valley, a very narrow one, hardly more than a large cleft between peaks. Pegasus swooped down into the pass, flying between two walls of snow—going more and more slowly, allowing the monster to catch up.

They reached the narrowest part of the pass. They were hemmed by walls of snow. Pegasus turned. The monster came toward them, spitting fire. In the thin mountain air its breath burned blue. Suddenly Pegasus folded his golden wings and dropped straight down. The Chimaera folded its leathery wings and dropped after them. Down, down, fell horse and rider until they were just above the valley floor.

Then, Bellerophon unslung the string of helmets he had made into a great rattle. He swung it about his head, sending a clamor into the still air, a horrid clanging din that doubled and redoubled itself as it bounced off the mountain walls.

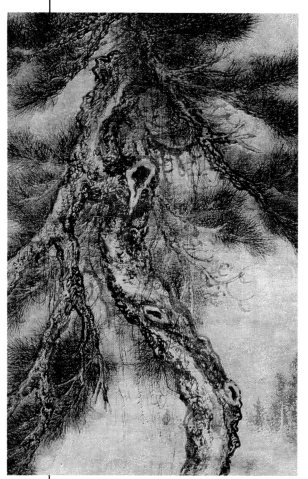

Pegasus dipped low over a pine tree.

Pegasus spread his wings again, caught a swell of air, and rose swiftly as the Chimaera was still dropping into the canyon. The monster, seeing them rise again, spread its wings also. But it could not soar like a gull. It had to beat its great leathery vans, trying to climb. By this time, the snow had begun to slide.

First it sounded like an enormous whisper. The whisper became a roar, then a thunderous, crashing, overwhelming noise as the sliding snow tore rocks out of their sockets, and the mountain walls literally collapsed, burying the Chimaera. Pegasus was almost caught by the avalanche, but just managed to fly high enough to avoid the plunging rocks. Even so, horse and rider were rimed with snow by the time they reached the level of the peaks.

Looking down, Bellerophon saw that the valley held a great mound of snow, a fitting grave, he thought, for so dreadful a monster. Then, aghast, he realized that he was savoring victory too soon. For the mound was melting, melting fast; it became a great lake of water even as he watched. The Chimaera's flaming breath had melted the snow. And the creature, he knew, being born of sea monsters, was at home in the water.

Horse and rider hovered above the new lake until they saw the Chimaera's head poke out. It was trying to climb out of the water and fly after its enemy, but it had to float for a while, regaining its strength.

"We can't let it fly," Bellerophon told his steed. "Once in the air, it will catch us, for its endurance is greater than ours. But there's one last thing we can try."

Pegasus understood. He tilted in the air and dove toward the lake. As they plummeted, Bellerophon drew his sword, lay flat on his belly, and allowed himself to slide along the horse's neck, onto the horse's head.

The winged stallion dived toward the lion-headed monster like a great heron trying to spear a fish with its beak. But the beak was Bellerophon's sword. Headfirst, Pegasus dropped, straight toward the Chimaera, steering himself so that the sword entered the monster's one vulnerable spot, its eye. Into that glaring jelly plunged the blade, deeper, deeper, until the horse's head skidded off the lion's head, and Bellerophon's fist was pressed against the bleeding socket.

The point of the sword found the dim clenched brain. The Chimaera died, thrashing in agony. Horse and rider were flung into the icy lake. They swam about for a moment, cleansing themselves of blood. But Pegasus quickly flew up again, or they would have frozen stiff.

The Chimaera lay still, all except the serpent tail, which was still twitching. Then that too stopped.

"Back to Helicon!" shouted Bellerophon. And the stallion bugled, his warm breath turning to mist.

They flew back to the mountain of the Muses, and there Bellerophon told Thallo two tales, as he had promised: one about his life in the court of Melicertes, the other about his battle with the Chimaera. And the little poet listened hungrily.

Bellerophon built a fire and sat as close to it as he could. He couldn't seem to get warm enough. Pegasus stood close too,

This was the first Centaur . . . who
galloped off with the young widow, Anteia.

sleeping on his feet, golden wings and mane gleaming in the firelight.

In the morning, Bellerophon bade Thallo farewell. "Where to now, my young hero?" asked Thallo.

"To Tiryns, to claim my reward—the fairest Anteia."

"Then you will have other adventures," said the poet, "for her husband will not yield easily. Will you come again, and tell me what happened?"

"I'll try," said Bellerophon. He mounted Pegasus and flew away.

Thallo never saw Bellerophon again but didn't much care. He had heard enough to fashion a new ballad. He knew that it was the best thing he had ever done, and grew so happy that he almost forgot the pain of his crippled legs. He had tried several endings to his poem before finding the right one. But he liked each of them in its own way and kept them all.

For in Thallo's song, Bellerophon, flying toward Tiryns, grew drunk with pride and joy and suddenly decided that he, as a son of Poseidon, should pay a visit to his high relatives—should fly up to Mount Olympus and tell his great deeds to his uncle Zeus and aunt Hera. Yes, he would meet the brawling Ares and the wing-footed Hermes, so that they might be proud of their kinsman from Corinth.

But Zeus, looking down from his great height and seeing a mortal flying toward heaven on the back of a magnificent golden-winged stallion, thought to himself, "This is what I've always feared—a mortal grown so arrogant that he wants to storm Olympus."

But according to the song, the angry god did not hurl his thunderbolt. He dispatched a gadfly instead. It was as large as a crow, with a sting like a dagger. It flew down and stung Pegasus under the tail. The horse bucked violently, and Bellerophon, whose pride had made him slack in the saddle, was thrown.

Down, down, he fell. When he hit the ground, he, like Thallo, shattered both legs.

Knowing that he was crippled for life, he dragged himself toward a forest, hoping to be eaten by a wild beast. But the faithful Sea Mist, who for many weeks had roamed the plains, waiting for his beloved master to return, found Bellerophon before he reached the wood. Nickering softly, he knelt so that the broken hero could climb upon his back.

A strange tale began to spread among the shepherds and farmers of Thessaly—a tale of a great gray stallion with a rider who never dismounted. The tale swelled, as years passed, into the legend of a creature half human, half horse, with the head and chest of a man and the body and legs of a horse. This was the first Centaur—and the tale told that it galloped to Tiryns, caught Proetus out hunting, kicked him to death, and galloped off with the young widow, Anteia. And she became the mother of the Centaur tribe, and their queen.

Acknowledgments

Letter Cap Illustrations by Hrana L. Janto

Opposite page 1, CHIMERA *(frontal view) (1983/86) by Mary Frank, papier mâché sculpture*
  Courtesy Zabriskie Gallery, New York

Page 2, THE LARGE BLUE HORSES *by Franz Marc (1880–1916), oil painting*
  Courtesy Walker Art Center Minneapolis; Gift of the T. B. Walker Foundation, Gilbert M. Walker Fund, 1942

Page 4, HEAD FROM AN ANTEFIX *(c. 500 B.C.), Etruscan painted terracotta*
  Courtesy Dallas Museum of Fine Arts; Foundation for the Arts Collection, anonymous gift in honor of Melba Whatley
    Photo: David Wharton

Page 7, WAR OR THE RIDE OF DISCORD, *by Henri Rousseau (1844–1920), oil painting*
  Courtesy of Jeu de Paume, Paris
    Photo: Scala/Art Resource, New York

Page 8, PORTRAIT OF A BOY *(Roman Period/2nd century A.D.), encaustic on wood, Egyptian from Fayum*
  Courtesy The Metropolitan Museum of Art, New York; gift of Edward S. Harkness, 1918

Page 10, RACING WITH THE MOON *(1986) by Juane Quick-To-See Smith, pastel drawing*
  Courtesy Bernice Steinbaum Gallery, New York

Page 12, MOUNTAINS AT COLLIOURE *by André Derain (1880–1954), oil painting*
  Courtesy National Gallery of Art, Washington, D.C.; John Hay Whitney Collection

Page 14, HORSE AND RIDER *by Marino Marini (1901–1980), bronze sculpture*
  Courtesy Hirshhorn Museum and Sculpture Garden, Smithsonian Institution, Washington, D.C.; gift of Joseph H. Hirshhorn, 1966
    Photo: John Tennant

Page 16, MADONNA *(1895–1902) by Edvard Munch, lithograph printed in color, composition (23 ¾ × 17 ½")*
  Courtesy The Museum of Modern Art, New York; the William B. Jaffe and Evelyn A. J. Hall Collection

Page 20, BOULDER—ROCKY LANDSCAPE *by Max Beckmann (1884–1950), oil painting*
  Courtesy The St. Louis Art Museum; bequest of Morton D. May

Page 22, PORTRAIT OF A MAN WITH DIADEM *(Roman Period/150–161 A.D.), encaustic on wood, Egyptian from Fayum*
  Courtesy The Metropolitan Museum of Art, New York; Rogers Fund, 1909

Page 24, TORMENTED MAN *(1956) by Leonard Baskin, ink drawing (39 ½ × 26 ½")*
  Courtesy Whitney Museum of American Art, New York; purchase with funds from the Living Arts Foundation Fund

Page 27, THE FIRST STEP *(1910–13? Dated on painting 1909) by František Kupka, oil painting on canvas (34 ¾ × 51")*
  Courtesy The Museum of Modern Art, New York; Hillman Periodicals Fund

Page 28, RISHI CALLING UP A STORM *by John La Farge (1835–1910), watercolor*
  Courtesy The Cleveland Museum of Art; J. H. Wade Fund

Page 30, WAR HELMET (TLINGIT) *(19th century), carved wood mask from Southeast Alaska*
  Courtesy Department of Library Services (No. 1928(2)), American Museum of Natural History, New York

Page 32, PANATHENAIC PRIZE AMPHORA *(detail of a horse race) (c. 510 B.C.), Attic: attributed to the Leagros Group*
  Courtesy The Metropolitan Museum of Art, New York; Rogers Fund, 1967

Page 34, PONTIAC *(1979) by Susan Rothenberg, flashe and acrylic painting*
  Courtesy Miani Johnson

Page 36, LI RIVER *(1985) by Wendy Edwards*
  Collection of the artist, Courtesy Fervor Gallery, New York

Page 38, HORSE *(8th century B.C.), bronze statuette, Greek*
  Courtesy The Metropolitan Museum of Art, New York; Rogers Fund, 1921

Page 41, ME AND THE MOON *by Arthur Dove (1880–1946), painting*
  Courtesy of The Phillips Collection, Washington, D.C.

Page 43, DOOR WITH COUCH–GRASS *(1957) by Jean Dubuffet, oil painting with assemblage*
  Courtesy Solomon R. Guggenheim Museum, New York
      Photo: David Heald

Page 44, UNTITLED *(1983–84) by Mary Frank, monoprint*
  Courtesy Zabriskie Gallery, New York

Page 46, EVOCATION OF BUTTERFLIES *(1910–12) by Odilon Redon, oil painting (21 ¾ × 16 ¼")*
  Courtesy The Detroit Institute of Arts; City of Detroit purchase

Page 48, HEAD OF VENUS *(mid-1st century A.D.), fresco painting from Pompeii*
  Courtesy The Bettmann Archive

Page 51, BRIDAL PAIR *(c. 1470) by anonymous South German master, oil painting on panel*
  Courtesy The Cleveland Museum of Art; purchase, Dalia E. Holden Fund and L. E. Holden Fund

Page 52, ETIENNE-MARTIN *(1956) by Karel Appel, oil painting (76 ⅞ × 51 ¼")*
  Courtesy The Museum of Modern Art, New York; purchase

Page 54, THE LITTLE COURIER *by Albrecht Dürer (1471–1528), engraving*
  Courtesy National Gallery of Art, Washington, D.C.; Rosenwald Collection

Page 56, THE RIDER ASLEEP *(1982) by Betsy Rosenwald, pastel drawing*
Private Collection, Courtesy the artist

Page 58, ON A LEE SHORE *by Winslow Homer (1836–1910), oil painting*
Courtesy Museum of Art, Rhode Island School of Design, Providence; Jesse Metcalf Fund

Page 61, BEACH—WELLFLEET *(1952) by Edwin Dickinson, oil painting on board*
Courtesy Graham Gallery, New York

Page 62, OUT OF THE BLUE *(1985) by Richard Bosman, oil painting*
Collection Gerald S. Elliott, Chicago, Courtesy Brooke Alexander, New York

Page 64, HOMO BEEF *(1983) by Luis Cruz Azaceta, acrylic and chalk drawing*
Courtesy Allan Frumkin Gallery, New York
Photo: eeva-inkeri

Page 66, VIOLET MOONLIGHT II *(1935) by Christian Rohlfs, watercolor (30 × 21 ½")*
Courtesy The Detroit Institute of Arts; gift of John S. Newberry, Jr., in memory of Dr. Wilhelm R. Valentiner

Page 68, THE COLT *by Georges Seurat (1859–1891), drawing*
Courtesy The Metropolitan Museum of Art, New York; Robert Lehman Collection, 1975

Page 70, PEGASUS AND BELLEROPHON *(19th century) by Odilon Redon, charcoal drawing*
Courtesy The Metropolitan Museum of Art, New York; Robert Lehman Collection, 1975

Page 73, THE BATHERS *by Paul Cézanne (1839–1906), color lithograph*
Courtesy The Metropolitan Museum of Art, New York; Rogers Fund, 1922

Page 75, BELLEROPHON ON PEGASUS *by Walter Crane (1845–1915), color drawing*
Courtesy The Bettmann Archive

Page 78, RAVINE *(1986) by Richard Bosman, oil painting*
Courtesy Brooke Alexander, New York

Page 80, BELLEROPHON KILLING THE CHIMAERA *by anonymous artist, copper engraving*
Courtesy The Bettmann Archive

Page 82, VULTURES ON A TREE *by Antoine-Louis Barye (1795–1875), watercolor and gouache drawing*
Courtesy The Metropolitan Museum of Art, New York; bequest of Mrs. H. O. Havemeyer, 1929. The H. O. Havemeyer Collection
Photo: Bob Hanson

Page 85, BELLEROPHON I *(1984) by Earl Staley, acrylic painting*
Private Collection, New York, Courtesy of the artist

Page 86, PINE TREE *(detail) (late 14th to 15th century) by Wu Po-li, hanging scroll*
Courtesy The Metropolitan Museum of Art, New York; gift of Douglas Dillon, 1984

Page 88, NESSUS AND DEIANIRA *(1920) by Pablo Picasso, pencil drawing (8 ¼ × 10 ¼")*
Courtesy The Museum of Modern Art, New York; acquired through the Lillie P. Bliss Bequest

BOOKS BY BERNARD EVSLIN

Merchants of Venus
Heroes, Gods and Monsters of the Greek Myths
Greeks Bearing Gifts: The Epics of Achilles and Ulysses
The Dolphin Rider
Gods, Demigods and Demons
The Green Hero
Heraclea
Signs & Wonders: Tales of the Old Testament
Hercules
Jason and the Argonauts